# CONISTON

Keith Wood

First published in Great Britain in 2010

British Library Cataloguing-in-Publication Data
A CIP record for this title is available from the British Library

ISBN 978 1 906887 78 0


**PiXZ Books**
Halsgrove House, Ryelands Industrial Estate,
Bagley Road, Wellington, Somerset TA21 9PZ
Tel: 01823 653777
Fax: 01823 216796
email: sales@halsgrove.com

An imprint of Halstar Ltd, part of the Halsgrove group of companies
Information on all Halsgrove titles is available at: www.halsgrove.com


Printed and bound in China by Toppan Leefung Printing Ltd

# Contents

# How to use this book

Coniston, famous for Ruskin, Donald Campbell and latterly Bluebird Bitter, offers great walking opportunities for either the experienced fell-walker or those seeking a more gentle stroll at lower levels amongst its spectacular and varied scenery. Although the key tourist spots of Coniston Village and the nearby Hawkshead can be busy at peak times, quiet footpaths and bridleways are quickly reached and the tranquillity of the area can be truly appreciated.

Overlooking the village of Coniston and the lake is an area of ground consistently over 2000 feet high known as the Coniston Fells. These Coniston Fells are scarred and pock-marked from mining and quarrying activity. In the eighteenth and nineteenth centuries this must have been a frightful, noisy and dirty place with smoke and fumes belching from the smelt mills above the village. Now all is quiet and the most likely disturbance is a group of walkers with their boots pounding along the old mine and quarry tracks.

One of Coniston Water's most popular attractions is the Coniston Launches which provide trips around the lake from Coniston Village (Walk 3 makes use of the service from Sunny Bank back to Coniston). The launches operate throughout the seasons; full details including timetables and special events are available from Coniston Launches, Coniston 017687 75753; www.conistonlaunch.co.uk

The majority of walks in this book are relatively easy to moderate and offer pleasant walking in this beautiful landscape. For the more adventurous, climbs up to Dow Crag, Coniston Old Man and Levers Water in Walks 4 and 5 give a taste of true, mountain walking.

Each route is graded from Easy to More Challenging with further details of distance, height ascended and the type of terrain covered, to help with decisions of which walk to choose. Each walk has details of refreshments and facilities available.

All ten walks are covered by the Ordnance Survey Explorer maps OL6: The English Lakes, South-Western area, and OL7: The English Lakes, South-Eastern area and Harvey's Lakeland South West and Lakeland South East maps. The maps in this book are only an outline version of each walk and the detail provided by the OS maps puts each route in context.

Every year tens of thousands of visitors enjoy the fells with the vast majority coming to no harm. However there are many cases each year where walkers are injured, get lost or find themselves in some other kind difficulty requiring the assistance of the Mountain Rescue Services. A few simple precautions should help avoid any problems:

- If you are unsure about your fitness start with the walks graded Easy and work your way up to More Challenging.
- Wear suitable footwear – properly fitted walking boots are recommended for all the walks.
- Take suitable clothing; the weather in the Lake District can change very quickly, take a waterproof and extra warm layers to wear.
- Take plenty to eat and drink en route, dehydration and lack of nourishment can lead to fatigue and mistakes being made.
- An outline map illustrates each walk but it is recommended that a complete map is taken.
- Inform someone of your planned route and expected return time.
- Check the weather forecast in advance and only take to the more challenging routes on clear days.
- And finally keep to the paths and watch where you are putting your feet – most accidents are caused by careless slips!

Useful websites:
Lake District National Park
www.lake-district.gov.uk
National Trust
www.nationaltrust.org.uk
Friends of the Lake District
www.fld.org.uk
Cumbria Tourism
www.golakes.co.uk
Lake District Outdoors
www.lakedistrictoutdoors.co.uk
Keith Wood Photography
www.keithwoodphotography.co.uk

## Key to Symbols Used

### Level of difficulty:

Easy

Fair 🌿 🌿

More challenging 🌿 🌿 🌿

### Map symbols:

🚗    Park & start

────    Tarred Road

- - - -    Footpath

■    Building / Town

+    Church

🪣    Pub

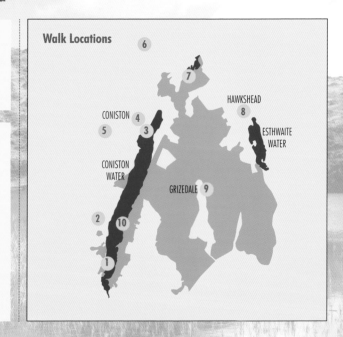

**Walk Locations**

CONISTON

HAWKSHEAD

ESTHWAITE WATER

CONISTON WATER

GRIZEDALE

# 1 Beacon Fell and Tarn

*An ideal start: a tarn, a fell and views of Coniston Water*

1000 m

Being the first walk in the book, this route serves as ideal introduction to the walking around Coniston Water; easy walking, great views and a host of little gems to discover. So whilst this may not be the toughest route ever walked by man it is full of delights; the reed edged Beacon Tarn, the little rocky summit of Beacon Fell and outstanding views of both the Coniston Fells and a full length view of Coniston Water.

**Level:** 🐾 🐾
**Length:** 4 miles (6.4km)
**Ascent feet and m:** 880 ft (265m)
**Terrain:** Easy road walking and clear Lake District paths
**Park and Start:** LDNP Brown Howe Car Park on A5084 south of Torver (Grid ref 289 910)
**Info:** Toilets at start

*The turn off from the road*

*Coniston Old Man across Torver Common*

**1** Park in the LDNP Brown Howe Car Park on the A5084 south of Torver. Head back onto the road and turn left, after 50 yards turn right onto the very narrow surfaced lane heading across Blawith Common. The common is covered in bracken and gorse sprinkled with silver birch trees. The lane meanders across Blawith Common gently rising to the Blawith Fells. As the road swings around to the right ignore a path off to the left. Stable Harvey Farm comes into view on the hillside to the right over a wall. Further along the road zig zags past a copse of trees on the right and crosses over Black Beck. As the road swings around to the right the views open out bringing the Coniston Fells into sight to the north in the distance.

**2** A Public Bridleway sign directs you to the left signed Cumbria Way onto a path following the Cumbria Way across the common heading towards Beacon Tarn. A wide green path keeps to the slightly higher ground out of the marshes on either side. Cross over Black Beck and take the lower of the two paths which heads along the edge of the marsh and then can be seen gently rising up the fellside and into the valley along which the tarn will be found. The path rises along the lower flanks of Beacon

*The first unnamed tarn*

the bog and the path can be seen rising again in the distance. Having passed the marsh the path rises again and the views start to open out to the south.

 Before too long Beacon Tarn comes into sight just below;

Fell with an outstanding view to the right of the Coniston Fells; Dow Crag, Coniston Old Man in the middle and Wetherlam to the right. The path swings around to the left and enters a valley with Beacon Fell on the left. The path levels off and passes on the left hand side of a large marsh and a small patch of water which must have been quite a large tarn at one time in the past. Continue along the edge of

head down towards the northern end of the tarn where the path forks; take the right hand path to walk around the western shore of the tarn. Keep to the path which hugs the shoreline which can be wet in places after rain and look back across the tarn to the top of Beacon Fell above the tarn.

*Beacon Tarn*

Beacon Tarn is an idyllic location on a summer's day with its reed beds, wild fowl and copse of trees. Cross the outflow of the tarn and continue walking around the tarn heading back north where the clear path heading up onto the top of the fell soon comes into view.

*Beacon Fell across Beacon Tarn*

(4) Leaving the tarn behind the wide green path starts to climb the fellside between the bracken. After an initial climb the path levels off and the top ridge of the fell can be seen ahead. The path drops down a short distance before climbing again, and after a final pull nearing the top a faint path darts off to the right to gain the summit ridge. Continue along the summit ridge where there is an excellent view of the tarn. All of a sudden the rocky top is reached with its large cairn and the views open out to the north to the Coniston Fells with Torver Tarn in the foreground and a full length view along Coniston Water to the right.

(5) The route continues heading north on the wide green path immediately losing height down the

*Pioneered by members of the Ramblers' Association in the 1970s, the Cumbria Way is a long distance footpath of 75 miles from Ulverston in the South to Carlisle in the North, passing through the varied and beautiful landscapes of the Lake District. Sections of the trail are followed on walks 1,2,3 and 7.*

fellside with the views to the foreground all the way down. After a steepish descent the path levels off and then forks, take the left fork which heads back to the narrow lane below. The path continues losing height all the while with Coniston Old Man directly ahead in the distance.

**6** Just before reaching the lane the electricity pylons which run across Torver Common are reached and an impressive lonely holly tree is passed. The path arrives back at the surfaced lane and so all that is required is to retrace the outward route along the road back to the start.

*Coniston Fells from summit of Beacon Fell*

# 2 **Torver Back Common**

*Water, water, everywhere; three tarns, a stream, a beck and Coniston Water itself*

This walk beside Coniston Water is a watery wonderland passing two tarns, a disused reservoir (commonly viewed as a tarn nowadays and so that makes three!), an unnamed stream, Torver Beck and of course Coniston Water itself. The walking is easy on clear paths including covering a stretch of the Cumbria Way – albeit in reverse to the most popular way of south to north.

**Level:** 🐾 🐾
**Length:** 3.75 miles (6km)
**Ascent feet and m:** 650' (200m)
**Terrain:** Mixture of clear paths, faint paths, couple of gentle uphill sections
**Park and Start:** Opposite the Land Rover Garage on the A5084, outside Torver (Grid ref 287 931)
**Info:** No facilities on route

*Coniston Water*

① Start from the Lakeland Land Rover Garage just to the south of Torver on the A5084 where there is ample parking opposite the garage. Leave on the track at the top corner of the car park opposite the garage with a sign "Farm Track Please Keep Clear". Pass through the gate at the end of the short track to enter the Lake District National Park's Torver Commons and take the green path heading off to the left. After a short distance the first tarn is reached. After pausing to take a look at Kelly Hall Tarn with its reed beds and lilies which make a great foreground to the view across to the Coniston Fells continue on the green path past the tarn heading north towards Coniston over the common. The path gently rises following the line of a drystone wall on the left. As

the wall turns sharply to the left the path forks with Long Moss Tarn straight ahead, take the left hand fork to keep walking on the clear path over Torver

Common. The path climbs an unnamed grassy knoll and then continues over higher ground onto a second knoll with a drystone wall just ahead.

*Kelly Hall Tarn*

2 From of the top of the knoll a grassy path leads downhill to the right, heading down towards Coniston Water with the drystone wall on the left. The path loses height as Coniston Water comes into view and a row of trees now accompanies the wall on the way down. The clear path heads down along the edge of Torver Common and enters a juniper jungle. The path gets closer to the wall now with a stream running in front, where the path forks keep to the right on the right hand bank of the stream. Follow the stream down through light woodland with silver birch and where the path splits into two tracks take the right track through a gate which then continues to head down through the woodland with the stream on the left. The tracks forks again and this time continue heading down beside the stream on the left hand track. The woodland path finally descends through the deciduous trees to join the main lakeshore path.

*Donald Campbell tragically died on Coniston Water in 1967 whilst breaking the water speed record in his boat Bluebird. The craft was recovered in 2001 and Campbell's remains interred in Coniston Cemetery. A prolific record breaker, an exhibition of Campbell's life is a permanent feature at the Ruskin Museum in Coniston.*

*Coniston Old Man from the Common*

3   Turn right to follow the lakeshore path along the banks of Coniston Water following the route of the Cumbria Way. It's just delightful easy walking along the tree-lined shore of the lake passing by little coves and the odd stream which trickles into the lake. As the path

leaves the trees and enters a second juniper jungle the Top O' Selside is seen on the opposite bank of the lake.

4   The path arrives at the Sunny Bank Jetty of the Coniston Launches after nearly a mile of walking and now the path veers to the right

and starts to climb through the bracken away from the lakeshore. Shortly the path is joined by a drystone wall enclosing woodland and continues heading up towards the road. Where the path forks, take the right hand path continuing to rise towards a wall up on the right, through a gate and the path continues through the bracken to shortly arrive at the road. The Coniston Fells come back into view on the right and Anne Riggs is the small hill straight ahead. Cross straight over the road and follow the Public Footpath sign and waymarker for the Cumbria Way through a kissing gate and take the path down to Torver Beck. Cross the wooden footbridge over the beck. The path rises following the depression beside Anne Riggs with a stream below on the left. The path

*Woodland path to the shoreline*

follows a line of telegraph poles carrying electric cables overhead. At a natural bowl the path forks: either will take you to Torver Reservoir, but for ease take the right path which rises over the end of Anne Riggs to join the main Public Footpath beside the tarn.

**5** Turn right to follow the path along the eastern shore of the disused reservoir known as Torver Tarn. The path rises again as it passes the end of the tarn with the Coniston Fells well displayed over the end of the tarn. Follow the clear path around the back of Anne Riggs, where the start point comes into sight over on the right. The path drops down to go through a gate at the narrow end of an enclosure into a walled lane leaving Torver Common behind. Pass around the back of the buildings of Mill Bridge, over the bridge back over Torver Beck and onto an unsurfaced lane which will take you back up to the main road and the start.

*Torver Beck*

*Torver Tarn*

# 3 Coniston Shoreline

*A delightful stroll along the lakeshore returning on one of the lake's cruisers*

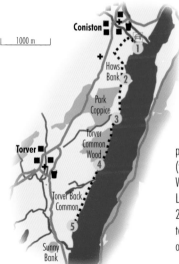

A ny visit to Coniston would be incomplete without taking a cruise on the lake or a walk along the lakeshore. This walk combines the two activities into a single enjoyable outing. Starting from the Coniston Boating Centre where there is ample parking the journey proceeds along the lakeshore path (following the route of the Cumbria Way) all the way to the Sunny Bank Landings jetty (also visited on Walk 2). To return you have the choice of taking the launch back to Coniston or to simply retrace your steps back

**Level:**
**Length:** 3.25 miles (5.2km)
**Ascent feet and m:** Negligible
**Terrain:** Easy walking on the level throughout
**Park and Start:** Coniston Boating Centre Car Park (Grid ref 307 970)
**Info:** Toilets at the start, refreshments from Coniston Village. Coniston Launch times: www.conistonlaunch.co.uk

along the lakeshore. Check the Coniston Launch website for sailing times before you set out. Look out for the National Trust's Steam Yacht Gondola along the way.

① Start from the LDNP Car Park at the Coniston Boating Centre just before the boat landings. Leave the Car Park and turn right to walk alongside the road initially heading back to the village of Coniston. Take the metal footbridge across the beck which is signed "Public Footpath Coniston 1/4 mile". Pass through the Lake Road Retail Estate and then turn left through the gates to pick up the Lakeshore Public Footpath to Torver along the route of the Cumbria Way Long Distance Trail. The well laid path makes its way along the edge of a couple of fields before turning sharply to the left across the middle of another field heading back towards the lakeshore and then turns to the right in line with the lakeshore to approach Coniston Hall.

*Coniston Hall*

② The path passes around the back of the historic Coniston Hall before resuming its way signed "Footpath Torver" on a surfaced track. The track makes its way through Coniston Hall Park and then through the middle of the campsite at Water Park. The route leaves Water Park onto the unsurfaced lakeshore path aided by a yellow waymarker arrow. Brantwood, Ruskin's home, can be seen on the opposite shore of the lake.

③ Cross the wooden footbridge over Hoathwaite Beck and keep straight on following the shoreline path. The quarry-scarred face of Coniston Old Man can be seen away on the right. Passing Hoathwaite Landing the path enters Torver Commons with its tree-lined path

*Coniston Old Man*

*Overlooking the lake with spectacular views of Coniston Old Man, Brantwood is the former home of John Ruskin. A radical voice in Victorian society, Ruskin was associated with the Pre-Raphaelite and Arts and Crafts Movements and inspired the founding of the National Trust and the Welfare State.*

along the edge of Torver Common with its traditional English mixed deciduous woodland of oak, beech and birch. The path passes Torver Landing Stage for the Coniston Launch before entering a stand of fir trees.

(4) Passing through a gate through a wall the path meets up with the section of the shoreline path also used on Walk 2. Just continue along the tree lined shore path down to Sunny Bank.

(5) Reaching Sunny Bank Landings there is the choice of picking up the twice daily boat to Coniston or retracing the outbound route back to Coniston.

*Torver Common*

*Steam Yacht Gondola*

# 4 **Coniston Coppermines Valley**

*A chance to explore Coniston's industrial heritage and visit a high level tarn*

Originally a natural tarn created by glacial activity in the last ice age, Levers Water's level was raised by a dam to provide a more controlled level of water for use by the mining industry below in the aptly named Coppermines Valley. At a height of 1355 feet (415m) it's quite a climb from Coniston itself, although you do get the added benefit of passing a host of waterfalls on the way which culminate in a spectacular triple decker falling directly out of the tarn itself. Now a place of leisure and tranquillity the Coppermines Valley was a scene of industrial activity for over

**Level:** 🐾 🐾 🐾
**Length:** 4.5 miles (7km)
**Ascent feet and m:** 1400' (425m)
**Terrain:** Clear paths throughout with a steep climb up to Levers Water
**Park and Start:** Coniston Information Centre Car Park (Grid ref 303 975)
**Info:** Toilets at the start, refreshments in Coniston

300 years with the mines and associated dressing and smelt mills belching fumes into the atmosphere. The walk passes plenty of evidence of mining activity along the way including a number of open levels; Do not be tempted to enter any of these – this is strictly a surface expedition!

*Levers Water*
*Coniston Fells*
*Raven Tor*
*Mines (disused)*
*Low Water*
*The Old Man of Coniston*
*The Bell*
*Coniston*

1000 m

23

① Start from the Car Park outside the Tourist Information Centre in the middle of Coniston. Leave the Car Park and head left to walk through the village signed Coniston Old Man, passing by The Crown Hotel. Turn right onto "Yewdale Road", the main road through the village. Pass the Black Bull Hotel, which houses the Coniston Brewery famous for its Coniston Bitter, and then immediately take the road on the left signed Coniston Coppermines and Youth Hostel. The road passes the Ruskin Museum. Take care; watch out for cars whilst walking along this lane heading towards the Coppermines Valley. As the lane starts to rise it loses its surface and becomes a track signed Public Footpath Coppermines Valley. The lane keeps on steadily

*Falls beneath the Miners Bridge*

rising with the sound of Church Beck down on the left. The path passes the impressive falls just beneath The Miners Bridge, pass the bridge and continue along the right hand bank of Levers Water Beck approaching the Coppermines Valley. Pass another set

of falls just below the weir and then the view opens out along the Coppermines Valley with the beck running through the centre, Swirl How at the head of the valley and the distinctive white-painted Youth Hostel in the middle of the scene. In the summer the copper spoil heaps stand out against the green bracken, in the autumn the whole scene is burnished copper. Continue along the track and pass by the remains of the copper smelt mill with bowl-shaped slugs of black slag. The track takes you in front of the Youth Hostel and then crosses a spoil heap and starts to rise again. At a junction of tracks at the modern waterworks take the first path up to the right continuing to steadily rise to the stream which is the outflow from Levers Water.

*The Miners Bridge*

more serious fell walking to be found hereabouts. Upon reaching the dam holding back the waters of Levers Water take your time to enjoy this high level tarn with Great How Crags looking down onto the tarn.

*The Coniston mines became the largest and most profitable copper mines in the north. So productive that in 1858 a branch line from the Furness Railway was constructed doing away with the slow, laborious carting and boating of ore via Coniston Water. However copper mining in Lakeland declined in the 1880s when cheap imported ore was brought from foreign lands.*

**2** Arriving at the foot of the falls from Levers Water and further evidence of former industrial activity, cross over the wooden foot-bridge and immediately turn right up the narrow stony path which unerringly ascends beside the trio of waterfalls all the way up to Levers Water some 350 feet above. This is a fairly stiff steep climb giving a flavour of the

*Coppermines Valley*

out down to Coniston and Morecambe Bay and the path back down the valley can be clearly seen. The much clearer path starts to gradually

*Triple Decker Falls*

(3) From the top of the path beside the falls turn left and head along the clear path around the tarn which continues to rise beneath Brim Fell End. When the path forks take the left hand fork to rise away from the shore of the tarn. The path

passes by a fenced off open mine level and deep crevasse; look but don't explore. Just past the levels head up to the left rising on a faint green path away from the tarn. As this rise is crested the path becomes clearer on the ground, the view opens

descend passing boulders which have fallen down from the crags of Brim Fell. The village of Coniston comes into view as the path loses height and it's downhill all the way. Cross over the wooden footbridge over the stream which flows down from Low Water which is next to another enormous boulder. Continuing on, the path passes over the disused slate quarry sledway with a couple of slate pillars giving clues as to their origins.

(4) At a T junction of paths take the left hand path and almost immediately the path forks again and again take the left fork heading back down the valley. As the lower reaches of the valley are passed the path passes through a drystone-built sheepfold. With Church Beck now on

the left, the weir and the Miners Bridge are soon reached. Continue on the right hand bank of Church Beck down towards Coniston. The route passes into a tree-lined enclosed lane. Nearing the end the lane drops down and passes over a stream passing

through a field before going through the back of Dixon Ground Farm to emerge onto the Walna Scar Road at the Sun Hotel. All that is now required is to turn left and walk back down the road into the middle of Coniston.

*Levers Water*

*Mining heritage*

# 5 Coniston Old Man

*A true fell walk to the top of Coniston's grand Old Man*

Overlooking the village of Coniston and the lake is an area of ground consistently over 2000 feet high known as the Coniston Fells. This walk takes us to three of the major peaks of the group taking advantage of some of the old miners' roads and giving fine views down onto the four tarns lying diagonally across the group of fells. Starting along the famous Walna Scar Road between Coniston and

**Level:** 🥾 🥾 🥾
**Length:** 6.5 miles (10.5km)
**Ascent feet and m:** 2600' (800m)
**Terrain:** A challenging fell walk along clear paths with a steep descent
**Park and Start:** Walna Scar Road above Coniston (Grid ref 289 970)
**Info:** Too many opportunities for refreshments in Coniston to list! No facilities directly on the route.

Seathwaite in the adjacent Duddon Valley the route climbs over the narrow ridge of Brown Pike, Buck Pike reaching the summit of Dow Crag which overlooks Goat's Water. A rollercoaster dip leads back up to Brim Fell leaving The Old Man of Coniston himself for the finale.

Map labels:
- 4
- Low Water
- Dow Crag
- 3
- Goat's Water
- The Old Man of Coniston
- The Bell
- 5
- Buck Pile
- Blind Tarn
- Little Arrow Moor
- 1
- 2 Brown Pike
- Walna Scar Road

└─ 1000 m ─┘

① Park through the gate at the end of the surfaced lane along the Walna Scar Road where there is plenty of space. Take the direction of the signpost "Public Bridleway to Seathwaite 3 miles" following the track around Coniston Old Man. This is a great fast way into the mountains gently rising as you walk along the wide unsurfaced track that is the Walna Scar Road. Ignore the road up to the right to a quarry and the path marked as a direct assault up the Old Man, keeping to the main route here. Enjoy the wide open views to the south across Torver Common with a brief glimpse of Coniston Water. Walking around a corner Brown Pike comes into view for the first time as the road becomes rougher and rises with more certainty. As the road gains

*Walna Scar Road*

more height catch a first glimpse of Morecambe Bay and the Irish Sea. A huge pile of stones just over a stream marks the point where the path to Goats Water heads off to the right; the climbers' route for the craggies who

wish to enjoy themselves on Dow Crag. Keep to the track to shortly reach a delightful pack horse bridge over the outflow of Goat's Water later to become Torver Beck. Cross over the bridge, and as the track gently rises

*Goat's Water and Coniston Old Man*

views open out over Coniston and Morecambe Bay. The track becomes steeper now, zig zagging around Brown Pike with slate quarrying remains to the right. Approaching the top of the pass, pass by a small well-built shelter, just big enough to keep one person safe out of the weather-in emergencies.

*Shelter on Walna Scar Road*

**2** All of the sudden the top of the Walna Scar Road is reached and an amazing vista opens out to the west, across the Duddon Valley to Harter Fell with the Scafells in the distance. Sellafield is clearly seen with the Irish Sea in the background and on a clear day even the Isle of Man is in sight. From the top of the pass take the clear path to the right leading steeply to the summit of Brown Pike. From the summit it's a simple enough walk following the clear path along the ridgeline heading to Dow Crag. A few feet from the path Blind Tarn can be seen below to the

Coppermines Valley from Coniston Old Man

path leading down to Goat's Hause, before rising up the other side to Brim Fell and Coniston Old Man. Continue on the path loosing 500 feet of hard-won height down to Goat's Hause, before steeling yourself for the last pull of the day; 500 feet back up to the ridge with Brim Fell and the Old

*Two centuries before Wainwright, the Lakes gained popularity as a tourist destination through Thomas West's Guide to the Lakes published in 1778. In it West, a Jesuit priest, describes the landscape from 'viewing stations'. The book continued to be popular until 1820 when it was superseded by Wordsworth's Guide.*

right. A steepish climb leads over the intermediate summit of Buck Pike only to realise that there is still a further couple of hundred yards and another sharp pull to reach the true summit of Dow Crag.

(3) After a minor scramble requiring the use of hands to assist, the rocky summit of Dow Crag is reached; take care not to stray too close to the precipitous edge. The next section of the walk can now be clearly seen; the

Man. Keep to the clear path up the other side pausing occasionally for a breather and to look back across to appreciate the sheer cliff face of Dow Crag and the shape of the ridge along to Brown Pike. The path flattens out as the wide ridge linking Brim Fell and the Old Man is reached; swing around to the left to make the minor detour to visit the summit of Brim Fell.

*Summit of Brim Fell*

**4** The top of Brim Fell is quickly reached marked by a well-built cone-shaped summit cairn. Take your time here to appreciate the wide open views to the east down to Coniston, across to Windermere and Ambleside and over to Hellvellyn. On a clear day the Howgills and even the great flat top of Ingleborough in Yorkshire can be clearly made out. Now simply follow the broad flat ridge over short cropped turf for the $^1/2$ mile to reach the summit of Coniston Old Man. The impressive top of the Old Man at 2633' (803m) marked by a platform adorned with huge cairn and a nearby Ordnance Survey Post is quickly reached. The crowds coming up the tourist route from Coniston are likely to be met at this point. The return begins on the path descending steeply down to Low Water tarn some 800 feet below. The surface is rough and loose in places due to the thousands of boots which come this way each year but the quality of the path soon improves and the path zig zags its way down to the tarn. From the tarn continue on the main path down through the slate mines. Do NOT be tempted to go into any of the open levels – danger lies within.

5 At a large cairn below The Bell marking a junction of paths take the right path to walk the remaining three quarters of a mile along the level on the Quarry Road back to the start point.

O.S. column on summit of Old Man

# 6 Tilberthwaite Mines

*An opportunity to safely explore some of Coniston's mining heritage*

**Level:** 🥾 🥾
**Length:** 2.25 miles (3.6km)
**Ascent feet and m:** 775' (235m)
**Terrain:** Fairly steep ascent and descent on clear paths
**Park and Start:** Grid ref 306 009
**Info:** Toilets and refreshments back in Coniston

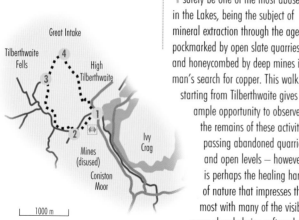

The area around Tilberthwaite must surely be one of the most abused in the Lakes, being the subject of mineral extraction through the ages; pockmarked by open slate quarries and honeycombed by deep mines in man's search for copper. This walk starting from Tilberthwaite gives ample opportunity to observe the remains of these activities passing abandoned quarries and open levels – however it is perhaps the healing hand of nature that impresses the most with many of the visible scars already being softened as plant life covers the evidence of earlier mining activity. As ever do not enter any of the open levels – danger lies within! The walk also gives an intimate inspection of Tilberthwaite Gill, the hidden bowl east of the bulk of Wetherlam and a surprise view of the Langdale Pikes.

The walk starts from beneath the slate quarry at Tilberthwaite, along the single track road off the A593, where there is plenty of roadside parking opposite one of Andy Goldsworthy's impressive

*Start here!*

sheepfold. Go up the slate steps onto the Tilberthwaite Gill access area beside a slate spoil heap on the right. The steps pop out onto the miners track which continues to rise steeply passing through the abandoned Penny

Rigg quarry workings. The track passes a huge slate spoil heap on the right and massive disused quarry pit on the left. The path levels off and the view along Tilberthwaite Gill opens out with Wetherlam at the head of the valley and the stream far below. The path continues to rise on up the valley. At the remains of a slate building the path forks; take the lower right hand path which heads along the level into the heart of the valley.

2 The path narrows and passes a stand of larch trees before dropping down to cross the gill over a wooden footbridge and then steeply climbs out of the ravine up the fellside on the opposite bank. Pass through a kissing gate and continue to rise straight up the fellside. The path joins

the main route along the northern side of the valley, turn left and head up the valley with the crags of Wetherlam ahead. The path levels off as the top of the gill is reached and as the falls at the top of the gill are passed the path starts to swing around to the right. Rounding the corner the path forks at a pile of stones; take the right hand fork. The path rises steadily on the outside rim of a great natural bowl towered over by the crags of Wetherlam. The remains of Tilberthwaite Coppermine are passed on the left. The path continue to rise passing by the boggy morass of Dry Cove Bottom. Keep to the main stony path around the edge of this natural bowl. Pass Dry Cove Moss; the furthest of the dark peat boggy areas below on the left as the path continues to rise.

Coppermines remains

*Leave the track here*

route continues straight ahead dropping down the slope to a wet valley; pass by the marshy area keeping the wire fence to your left hand side. As the path continues to descend down the fellside the best view of the day opens out to the north looking across Blea Tarn to the Langdale Pikes. Continue down the slope with fence on the left towards a junction of walls and a small wooden sheepfold.

*View from the highest point*

(3) At a copper-coloured slag heap, a large stone cairn and a derelict hut, leave the main path and turn right to head up the hillside on a faint path towards Hawk Rigg. Shortly pass by a fenced mine level where the path becomes clearer on the ground. Just past the level the depression between Hawk Rigg and Blake Rigg is reached marking the high point of the route just next to a little scrap of water where the view to the east opens out with extensive views to Helvellyn and Fairfield. The

*Langdale Pikes along Little Langdale*

junction of paths, where the beck crosses the path, turn left to drop down behind the buildings of High Tilberthwaite. Follow the unsurfaced track down to the road below. All that remains is to turn right and follow the road back to the start and an inspection of the Andy Goldsworthy sheepfold.

*'Sheepfolds' is a Cumbria-wide sculpture project by Andy Goldsworthy and has lead to the restoration of some 46 folds. Often neglected and in a state of disrepair, the folds are restored using traditional materials and techniques. The Tilberthwaite Touchstone Fold is a fine example of art in the environment.*

**4** At the bottom of the slope in front of the wall turn right and walk below the dry stonewall. Gradually the path becomes clearer on the ground. Simply keep following the well-built wall. Tilberthwaite soon appears below and the path starts to descend down to the valley below. Pass a stand of larches with the water in the ravine below on the right. A stile is crossed and the now green path continues to descend. At a

*Andy Goldsworthy Sheepfold*

# 7 Tarn Hows and Black Fell

*A circuit of the ever popular tarn with a climb to a nearby summit*

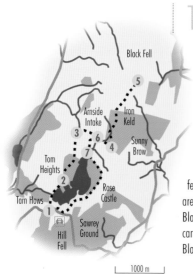

**Level:** 🥾 🥾
**Length:** 4 miles (6.4km)
**Ascent feet and m:** 900' (275m)
**Terrain:** Clear paths throughout with gentle ascent to the top of Black Fell
**Park and Start:** National Trust Car Park at the southern end of Tarn Hows (Grid ref 327 995)
**Info:** Toilets at the start

*Wetherlam from near the start*

The circuit around Tarn Hows must be one of the most popular short walks in the Lake District and justifiably so. However to make the walk a little more interesting (and challenging) combining the circuit with the ascent of the nearby Black Fell makes a much more satisfying excursion. There seems to be some dispute regarding the naming of this little fell, both Black Fell and Black Crag are in use – I've decided to go with Black Fell but having visited the top can equally see why it's known as Black Crag.

 Starting from the main National Trust Car Park at the southern end of Tarn Hows leave the Car Park and cross over the narrow lane onto the unsurfaced but well maintained paths around the tarn following the National Trust signs for the circular path around the tarn. Immediately on joining the dressed path a green path heads up to the left through the bracken to a viewpoint overlooking the Coniston Fells. It's worthwhile making this little detour before returning back down onto the dressed path. This circular is going to be clockwise around the tarn. At the first fork in the path take the right hand path which heads down to the shoreline. The path crosses over the outflow of the tarn. The path leaves the shoreline and proceeds

through the trees of the principally coniferous woodland which surround the western side of the tarn.

 At a traditional wooden walkers sign the path forks;

take the left hand path signed "Arnside and Langdales" heading away from the tarn along the route of the Cumbria Way long distance trail on a rocky path through the trees.

*Tarn Hows is one of the most visited spots in Lake District. Although beautiful, the current tarn is partly artificial, being three tarns joined together in the nineteenth century by the damming of the Lower Tarn. Bought by Beatrix Potter in 1929, she bequeathed the land to the National Trust.*

**3** Pass through a gate to emerge onto an unsurfaced walled lane with a minor tarn straight ahead; turn right at this junction sign-posted to Iron Keld and Hawkshead. This stony unsurfaced lane gently rises around the northern end of Tarn Hows before levelling off with occasional glimpses down to Tarn Hows on the right. Continue past a pair of gates on either side of the lane and continue along the lane as it bends around to the left.

**4** Approaching the top of another rise a clear path heads off through a wooden gate up to the left signed Public Bridleway "Iron Keld, Black Crag and Arnside". This stony path continues to gently rise heading towards Black Fell. The path rises through a bleak and barren area of harvested woodland and arrives at another junction of paths. Continue

*Turn right for Black Fell*

*View from Black Fell*

Black Crag is reached with its stone-built Ordnance Survey column. The panoramic view includes: to the north Dunmail Raise, east to Windermere, south Morecambe Bay, Tarn Hows, Coniston Water and the Coniston Fells and to the west Lingmoor, Bowfell and the Langdale Pikes. A hundred yards away from the summit to the south another well-built monumental cairn is reached which looks out over Windermere.

(5) Retrace your footsteps through the bracken back towards Tarn Hows. Go through the first gate and all the way back to the second gate which meets up with the walled lane and return to the right. The path around Tarn Hows can be seen through the tress to the left.

straight on following the sign to High Arnside which approaches a drystone wall. Go through the wooden gate through the wall and immediately take the path up to the right. This path takes you all the way to Black Fell on a narrow path which continues to rise across the fell. As the path levels off the view opens out to the north and the summit pillar of Black Fell can be seen straight ahead in the middle ground. Follow the path over the bracken for one last climb to reach the top. After a final stiff climb the top of

*Cairn looking to Windermere*

**7** Cross over a stile and turn left to complete the clockwise circuit of the tarn. Cross the wooden bridge over the stream which feeds into the top of the tarn and enjoy the full length view along the tarn. Simply walk along the dressed path which runs through the trees along the eastern shore of the tarn. The path climbs above the tarn again and at the last junction follow the path signed to Yewdale around the foot of the tarn and thence back to the start.

*Tarn Hows*

**6** Walk back to the pair of gates on either side of the walled lane and take the left hand gate through the wall to follow the narrow path through the bracken, guided by waymarker posts which take you down to meet up with the main dressed path around the tarn.

*Tarn Hows*

# 8 Latterbarrow

*A walk from the ever popular Hawkshead to a magnificent viewing station overlooking Lake Windermere*

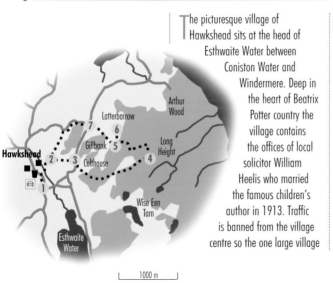

The picturesque village of Hawkshead sits at the head of Esthwaite Water between Coniston Water and Windermere. Deep in the heart of Beatrix Potter country the village contains the offices of local solicitor William Heelis who married the famous children's author in 1913. Traffic is banned from the village centre so the one large village

**Level:** 🐾 🐾
**Length:** 4.5 miles (7.2km)
**Ascent feet and m:** 750' (225m)
**Terrain:** Clear paths, some road walking and two gentle pulls on the way
**Park and Start:** Lake District National Park Car Park, Hawkshead (Grid ref 353 980)
**Info:** Toilets at start, refreshments from various outlets in Hawkshead

car park on the outskirts of the village is well signed. This walk to the local viewpoint of Latterbarrow with its enormous stone-built cairn gives plenty of opportunity to look back down onto Hawkshead with its distinctive whitewashed buildings.

47

Cross over the lane

Park in the main LDNP Car Park at Hawkshead. Leave the Car Park back onto the main road around the village turning left to walk on the pavement along North Lonsdale Road. As the road swings around to the left cross over and go down the lane on the right signed "Public Footpath Scar House Lane". Almost immediately the path forks; take the right fork signed "Public Footpath" along a narrow walled lane. Cross the footbridge over Black Beck and follow the path to the left around the field perimeter, and then through a wooden gate onto a green path which leads across the next field.

Cross over a stream and then immediately go though another wooden gate. Take the right hand path signed to Colt House on a clear but narrow path around the field margins. Pass through the kissing gate into an enclosed lane and go straight across the lane through a gate following the sign "Public Footpath Crofts Head and Claife Heights". The green path rises through this next field,

*Hawkshead from the way up*

head to the front right aiming for a stone-stepped wall stile marked by a yellow waymarker, climb over the wall into the next field and again follow the yellow waymarker pointing the way forward with the summit cairn of Latterbarrow in sight straight ahead on the horizon. Bear right across this field aiming for a gap in the wall (formerly a gateway) to walk around the back of a house with an iron fence and high hedge. Follow the yellow waymarkers through a wooden fence to arrive at a surfaced lane.

*Lily covered tarn*

Turn right to walk down the lane and at a T-junction turn left where after another 50 yards and just before the gates to Gillbank a wooden gate signed "Public Bridleway to Bell Grange and The Sawreys" doubles back on yourself leading up the hillside to the right. This unsurfaced lane immediately starts to rise and bends around to the left. The lane steadily rises giving views down onto the village of Hawkshead on the right. The stony lane continues rising. Pass through a gate through the deer fence and the route continues heading up the hillside. Keep to the main path through light woodland avoiding any temptations to veer off the path to left or right. The path levels off before passing another gate and continues to rise. Pass by an idyllic woodland tarn on the right covered in water lilies in the early summer. The track flattens off and then rises again through another gate. The views open out to the east across to the Fairfield Horseshoe and Kirkstone Pass.

*Beatrix Potter is best known as the author and illustrator of the children's book* The Tale of Peter Rabbit. *During her life she purchased farms and land in the Lake District, becoming an expert Herdwick Sheep breeder. On her death in 1943 she left 14 farms and 4000 acres of land to the National Trust.*

**4** At a gap in the wall a three directional signpost is reached, turn left signposted "Footpath Latterbarrow" on the clear path through the harvested woodland. The path drops down a dip and then passes through a wall. Once again follow the main path initially to the right along the wall which then swings to the left and again the impressive summit pillar of Latterbarrow comes into view. Keep the faith along the main path as it meanders through the bleak cropped woodland. The path eventually enters a plantation of mature pines, keep to the path along the edge of the plantation.

**5** Exit the woods over a stile to reach a signpost where the path forks; head up to the right signed "Latterbarrow". Walk up the last rise through the bracken to reach the summit of Latterbarrow.

*Windermere and the Fairfield Horseshoe from Latterbarrow*

**6** From the impressive summit pillar, there are panoramic views from Coniston Fells in the west to Ambleside and Windermere in the east. Having enjoyed the view head back down the bracken slopes to the corner of the woodland and now follow the sign right labelled "Hawkshead". The clear path gradually loses height heading down beside a boundary wall and fence. Down down all the way down for nearly 1/2 a mile.

**7** Emerge through a gate onto quiet surfaced lane, turn left and continue heading down the hill. After barely 20 yards turn right down the single-tracked Loanthwaite Lane continuing to lose height for another 600 yards down the lane. Just before reaching a typical Lakeland farm, take the second of the two signposts to the left directed to "Hawkshead Village via Scar House Lane". With Hawkshead in view the path goes along the edge of the field, passes through a kissing gate and heads down the edge of a second field. Pass through another kissing gate onto a narrow lane, follow this to the left for 50 yards before the sign "Public Footpath to Hawkshead" points the way through the next field to yet another kissing gate now with the church in view directly ahead. Finally join up with the outward route and just retrace your steps across the fields back to the start.

*Latterbarrow summit pillar*

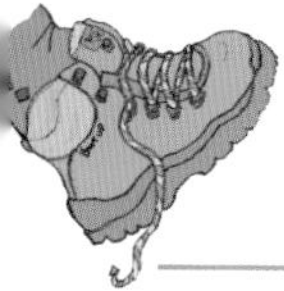

# 9 Carron Crag

*A walk through Grizedale Forest to the summit of Carron Crag*

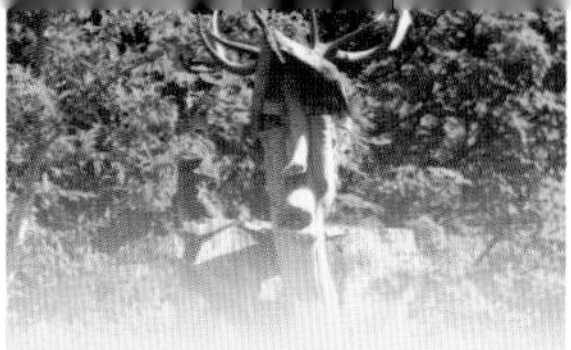

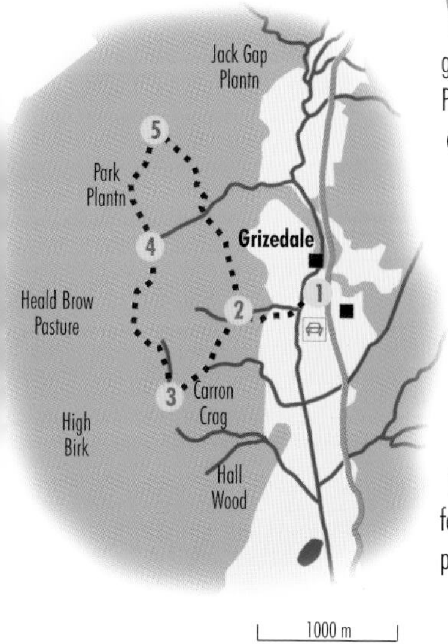
Jack Gap
Plantn
5
Park
Plantn
4
Grizedale
Heald Brow
Pasture
2
1
3
Carron
Crag
High
Birk
Hall
Wood
1000 m

Vast tracts of the fellside to the east of Coniston are covered in evergreen forest. This is Grizedale Forest Park covering some 2447 hectares or over 6000 acres in old money. With public access encouraged by the Forestry Commission, Grizedale has become something of an outdoor adventure playground with some eight waymarked walkers trails, five cycle trails and for the more adventurous "Go Ape" high level rope ways. Grizedale is also famous for its sculptures which can be found throughout the forest, principally made from a range of natural materials. The highest point in the forest overlooking Coniston is Carron Crag at 1030 feet or 314 m and it is the walk from the Forest Centre to the top of Carron Crag that is the most suitable for this collection of walks.

**Level:**
**Length:** 3 miles (4.8km)
**Ascent feet and m:** 750′ (225m)
**Terrain:** Well made forestry paths and tracks throughout
**Park and Start:** Grid ref 335 943
**Info:** Toilets and refreshments from the Grizedale Forest Centre.
www.forestry.gov.uk

① Park in one of the car parks at the Grizedale Forest Centre. From the Visitor Centre pass by the adventure playground and head for the door through the wall on the left. Go through the door in the wall and turn right to head down the lane following the multi-coloured trail markers. Actually it is the red trail markers which mark the whole of this route. Cross the bridge over the Grizedale Beck past the farm and as the road swings around to the right a footpath marked by green, red and yellow goes straight on to enter the forest. Immediately the path forks; take the right fork up the stepped path. The climb up through the trees to the top of Carron Crag begins initially gently rising on this forest path. Following the waymarkers the path

*The Ancient Forester at Grizedale Visitor Centre*

continues up the edge of the forest with a wall on the left.

② Arriving at a forest road turn right to walk along the road. At the first narrow path on the left, take it with its red marker and continue rising up the hillside through the forest. Rising through the conifer woodland the path emerges at a crossroads of tracks. Turn right along a forest road for 50 yards before turning left up the next narrow path marked by the ever present red and green marker.

③ This stony forest path continues to rise up between the trees. At the edge of the trees the first oval art installation '17° South' comes into view, quickly followed by the OS column which marks the top of Carron

*Sunlit fern in Grizedale Forest*

Crag. The view to the north and west dramatically opens out to Coniston Copper mines Valley with the Old Man, Swirl How and Wetherlam dominating the scene to the west. Despite this high vantage point with panoramic views the only water visible is Morecambe Bay to the south.

**(4)** Having paused to enjoy the extensive views the path continues over the top of the fell between the heather and bilberries heading north with the Helvellyn ridge in sight through the trees. The path shortly starts to descend back down into the trees. The path emerges to join another forest road with open views; turn left and continue following the red and green waymarkers. The road meanders through the upper areas of the harvested forest.

*Follow the waymarkers to the top*

*17° South Sculpture just before reaching the summit*

*For over 30 years, Grizedale Forest has been renowned for its forest sculptures. Started in 1977 by the Grizedale Society, over 90 sculptures made from natural materials have taken their place in the forest – the Visitor Centre dominated by the impressive 'Ancient Forester'. Sculptors have included Sally Matthews and Andy Goldsworthy.*

(5) Just as the forest road swings away to the left a narrow stony path heads down to the right back into the trees again marked by red/green posts. The path is now heading back in the direction of the Visitor Centre. Shortly the wide path starts to descend back through the trees. The path emerges onto another forest road; head right along the track. As the end of the route approaches retrace the initial stages of the walk leaving the road at the edge of the forest and heading back down the path to the Visitor Centre.

*Summit of Carron Crag*

*Walking in Grizedale Forest*

## 10 Top O' Selside

*A simple climb to the highest peak overlooking Coniston's eastern shore*

1000 m

Top O' Selside is the obvious place to complete our exploration around Coniston Water as it is the highest point to the east of the lake at 1091 feet or 335m. However easy and safe routes are harder to come by than seems obvious on the map, the area to the south east of the summit is a featureless soggy wilderness with few clear paths and a reasonable chance of ending up "off piste". The easiest route to follow is the one I've chosen starting from Dodgson Wood on the lakeshore, climbing through the trees and then walking along the

**Level:** 🥾 🥾
**Length:** 3 miles (4.8km)
**Ascent feet and m:** 950' (290m)
**Terrain:** Stiff climb up to Parkamoor, clear paths throughout
**Park and Start:** Grid ref 299 926
**Info:** No facilities on route

high level track above the lake. It means that it's a straight "there and back" route but the views in both directions whilst walking along the high level track are outstanding and serve as a perfect finale to this collection.

10

*Reflections in Coniston Water*

① Start from the National Trust's Dodgson Wood Car Park on the eastern side of Coniston Water. Leave on the stepped path at the back of the Car Park to head up to Low Parkamoor walking through the deciduous woodland of mainly oak trees. After barely a couple of hundred yards the path passes around a stone building used as a base for outdoor education activities before passing through a gate showing a Permissive Path to Low Parkamoor where a clear stony path starts to rise up the hillside through the woodland. Arriving at a forest track a white waymarker helpfully points the way to the left continuing to rise through the trees. As the track swings sharply to the left a white waymarker points to a narrow path on the right which crosses a fellside stream before continuing to rise again. Ignore the wooden gate through the fence on the left onto the open fellside but continue straight on through the upper edge of the wood. The path swings up to the left and through a gate leaving the wood behind on a clear narrow path which continues to rise following the line of a drystone wall on the left. Shortly the view opens out to the left down to Coniston Water and across to Torver Common and the Coniston High Fells beyond. With the lonely farmstead of

*Low Parkamoor*

Low Parkamoor on the left the path now follow the line of a beck to emerge on the fellside track with Parkamoor on the left.

(2) Turn right to walk along the high level track above the lake heading towards Selside. As the track continues to rise magnificent views come into sight; down onto Coniston Water and across to Torver Common and Sunny Bank Landing on the opposite shore. After a couple of hundred yards a three way junction comes into view; go straight on continuing on the clear track signed to High Nibthwaite. It's easy walking on this fine high level track above Coniston Water with Beacon Fell to the front right and shortly Peel Island made famous by Arthur Ransome's *Swallows and Amazons* comes into view.

(3) With the far end of the lake coming into sight and with Peel Island just below a wooden way-marker points up a green path up the fellside to the left. 50 yards up this green path a further narrow green

*The author Arthur Ransome is best known for his book series Swallows and Amazons, tales of idyllic childhood summers. Although he changed the names of houses and places in his books, fans are pretty sure that Peel Island on Coniston is the Wildcat Island of the stories.*

*Beacon Fell above Coniston Water*

*Foot of the lake*

summit cairn with the Helvellyn range to north east with Morecambe Bay to the south although Coniston Water itself is obscured by the moorland. Just to the east is the pretty Arnsbarrow Tarn which on a sunny day is worth a visit using the narrow trod away from the summit.

**4** To avoid getting lost in the wild and wet moorland beyond the summit simply resume the outbound journey back down to the woods. Back at the three way sign, don't forget that it's the left hand track to take to Parkamoor which heads down. Just before reaching the gate on the track to Parkamoor take the clear path back down on the left beside the stream heading back to the trees and down to the start.

path turns off to the left for the gentle climb up to the Top O' Selside. There are stunning views up the lake to the Coniston Fells on this short climb to the top. The path meanders up the hillside steadily rising to eventually arrive at the rocky Top O' Selside. There is a panoramic view from the